Emotional Intelligence Mastery: Constructing Your Path to Self-Understanding

Emotional Intelligence Mastery: Constructing Your Path to Self-Understanding

Copyright © 2023 by **Monday Farouq**

Table of content

INTRODUCTION   6

Why Emotional Intelligence Matters   7

The Pillars of Emotional Intelligence   8

Your Path to Emotional Intelligence Mastery   8

CHAPTER 1: UNDERSTANDING YOUR EMOTIONAL WORLD   10

The Nature and Purpose of Emotions   10

Components of Emotional Experiences   11

Individual Emotional Patterns   14

Investigating Your Emotional Patterns   15

Emotion-Provoking Beliefs   17

Activity: Identifying Your Emotion-Provoking Beliefs   18

Managing Emotion-Provoking Beliefs   19

The Mind-Emotion Connection   20

CHAPTER 2: MASTERING EMOTION REGULATION   23

The Costs of Poor Emotion Regulation   23

The Emotional Mind vs. Rational Mind   24

Change Negative Emotional Habits   27

Strategies to Regulate Difficult Emotions   28

Developing Emotional Agility   30

Turning Emotional Pain into Insight   31

CHAPTER 3: MOTIVATION THROUGH EMOTIONAL WISDOM   33

Fleeting Happiness From External Rewards   33

The Hedonic Treadmill of Material Success   34

Sources of Internal Motivation   35

Design a Life That Fills Your Spirit   37

Motivation From Flow States   38

Live Your Eulogy Today   40

CHAPTER 4: THE PATH TO EMPATHY   42

What is Empathy?   42

The Evolutionary Roots of Empathy   43

Obstacles to Empathy   44

Benefits of Empathy   44

Active Listening Techniques   45

Vulnerability Builds Bonds   46

The Empathetic Mindset   48

Develop Cognitive Empathy Through Reading   49

Loving-Kindness Meditation   50

CHAPTER 5: APPLY EMOTIONAL INTELLIGENCE OUTWARD   52

Emotional Intelligence Creates Effective Communication   52

Providing Constructive Feedback   53

Managing Interpersonal Conflict   54

Cultivating Influence and Inspiration   55

Emotional Intelligence Creates Compelling Stories   56

Complementing Success and Sacrifice   56

CHAPTER 6: YOUR EMOTIONAL INTELLIGENCE JOURNEY   59

Pathway to Mastery   59

Internalizing Key Emotional Skills   60

Daily Tools to Develop EQ   61

Long-Term EQ Goals to Set   62

Lifelong Development   63

CONCLUSION   66

Journey of Self-Discovery   66

Expanding Your Circle of Compassion   67

Live With Emotional Wisdom   68

ABOUT THE AUTHOR   69

Introduction

Emotional intelligence - the ability to understand, manage, and reason with emotions - is a critical skill for living a fulfilled, meaningful life. Those with high emotional intelligence are able to identify their own emotions and motivations, regulate their feelings and responses, empathize with others, and employ emotions in constructive ways. Extensive research has demonstrated that emotional intelligence is essential for personal well-being, strong relationships, academic and career success, leadership, and more.

Yet many people lack a solid grasp of their own emotions. We go through life on autopilot, reacting to situations and allowing our feelings to control us, rather than responding intentionally. This leads to rumination, impulsiveness, conflict, stress, and an inability to connect deeply with ourselves and others. Without a conscious awareness and mastery of our emotional landscape, we are like sailors lost at sea, without a compass to guide us.

This book provides that compass, laying out the key concepts, practices, and self-reflective tools to navigate the waters of your emotional world. Emotional intelligence is not an innate talent - it is a skill that can be deliberately cultivated through knowledge, self-awareness, and applied effort. By reading this book, you will be constructing your unique path to mastery based on proven frameworks and your own self-understanding.

Why Emotional Intelligence Matters

Emotions serve an important evolutionary function. They helped our ancestors survive by urging them to act in certain ways, like fleeing from danger or bonding with others. Today, we need our emotions to thrive, not just survive. Emotional intelligence enables us to use our emotions wisely so they facilitate rather than hinder our personal growth and goals.
Science has uncovered many benefits of having high emotional intelligence:

- Physical health - Managing stress and nurturing positive emotions contributes to biological health and longevity.
- Mental health - Understanding emotions mitigates anxiety, depression, rumination, and impulsiveness.
- Relationships - Emotionally intelligent people have stronger social skills and empathy to build fulfilling relationships.
- Career - EQ boosts leadership, motivation, teamwork, decision making, and performance.
- Life satisfaction - Perceiving emotions clearly and regulating them adaptively increases well-being and life satisfaction.

Without emotional intelligence, even people with high IQ can be ineffective in life because they lack the ability to handle emotions, connect with others, and motivate themselves. EQ serves as your internal GPS - helping you navigate all of life's challenges and opportunities.

The Pillars of Emotional Intelligence

There are five core competencies that make up emotional intelligence:

1. Emotional self-awareness - Understanding your own emotions, what triggers them, and their impact.
2. Emotion regulation - Handling feelings constructively rather than being controlled by them.
3. Internal motivation - Guiding yourself based on values rather than external validation.
4. Empathy - Recognizing emotions in others and relating with compassion.
5. Interpersonal skills - Managing emotions effectively in relationships and social interactions.

This book will provide research-backed techniques to help you master each of these pillars and integrate EQ skills into your daily life. While some people are naturally more emotionally adept, these competencies can be consciously cultivated through mindful effort.

Your Path to Emotional Intelligence Mastery

The journey to self-understanding requires self-reflection, courage, and persistence. This book will walk you through the process in a step-by-step manner:

- First, we will build emotional awareness by studying the nature of emotions, identifying your personal patterns, values, and triggers.

- Next, you will gain strategies to regulate unhelpful emotions and align your actions with your values to unlock internal motivation.
- Building empathy for others will further expand your EQ skills.
- Finally, you'll learn to employ your emotional intelligence to communicate effectively, manage conflict, and nurture all your relationships.

The path will not always be easy, but the rewards are immense. Each chapter ends with exercises to integrate the concepts, so you can actively practice while reading. By applying emotional intelligence across life domains, you will construct the specific abilities you need to thrive.

This journey is not about manipulating emotions or forcing yourself to feel certain ways. It is about objectively understanding your inner world - the beautiful diversity of your emotional landscape - so you can make conscious choices aligned with your values.

Imagine what life would be like if you responded thoughtfully rather than reacting impulsively. You can uncover that self-awareness and power - your compass is here. Let's begin charting your course to emotional intelligence mastery.

Chapter 1: Understanding Your Emotional World

Emotional intelligence starts with understanding your personal emotional world. This chapter will dive deep into the nature and purpose of emotions, patterns in your emotional life, and core beliefs driving your emotional experiences. With deeper self-awareness, you can begin to consciously shape your EQ journey.

The Nature and Purpose of Emotions

Emotions are automatic physical and psychological responses to internal and external events. They evolved to help our ancestors survive by prompting them to act quickly in the face of threats and opportunities.

For instance, fear would arise when facing a predator, signaling danger and preparing the body to fight or flee. Love and attachment would bring people together to care for infants and strengthen social bonds. Disgust discouraged eating rotten food. Joy rewarded beneficial experiences to motivate their repetition.

While primal emotions helped with basic survival, humans also developed self-conscious emotions that reflected our complex social needs. Emotions like shame, guilt, pride, and embarrassment arose to facilitate group norms and cooperation.

So, emotions serve many adaptive purposes:

- **Communication** - Emotions convey internal states and intentions to others through facial expressions, gestures, tone of voice, and body language. This facilitates social coordination and empathy.
- **Motivation** - Emotions focus attention on the most urgent concerns and drive us to act on them. They mobilize energy for meeting life's challenges.
- **Guidance** - Emotions highlight what is important and provide feedback on the potential value or harm of different situations and relationships.
- **Connection** - Shared emotional experiences strengthen social bonds and intimacy through empathy and mutual understanding.
- **Well-being** - Pleasant emotions like joy, excitement, love, and tranquility contribute to subjective well-being and life satisfaction.

Understanding the evolutionary purposes behind your emotions allows you to see them as useful sources of data, not as forces to be ignored or eliminated.

Components of Emotional Experiences

There are several key components that together produce subjective emotional experiences:

- **Cognitive appraisal** – The mental assessment and interpretation of the emotional trigger. For example, perceiving a situation as threatening lead to fear.

- **Physical reactions** - Emotions activate widespread bodily changes in the nervous system, face, vocal cords, muscles, heart rate, breathing, and hormones like adrenaline.
- **Feelings** - The subjective positive or negative qualities associated with the emotion like anger feels agitating, sadness feels heavy.
- **Action urges** - Each emotion motivates typical behavioral reactions - anger makes us want to attack, fear makes us want to escape/avoid, joy makes us want to join in.
- **Names and labels** - The words, facial expressions, gestures, and metaphors used to represent and communicate the emotion.

By breaking down the components involved in forming emotions, you can better understand the complexity behind your subjective emotional experiences. This also reveals how you can intervene in shaping emotions.

Primary Emotions

There are considered to be 6-10 primary, universal emotions experienced to some degree by all humans:

- Happiness - Joy, excitement, contentment, pride.
- Sadness - Grief, shame, despair, feelings of loss.
- Anger - Annoyance, rage, frustration.
- Fear - Anxiety, nervousness, unease, restlessness.
- Disgust - Revulsion, contempt, distaste.
- Surprise - Shock, astonishment, amazement.

Additionally, interest and trust are sometimes considered fundamental emotions. All other emotions arise from combinations of these primal emotions or exist on a spectrum between them. For example, irritation contains elements of anger, disgust, and fear.

Understanding the primary emotions provides a useful framework to categorize the rich diversity of your emotional experiences. It also reveals patterns in how you respond emotionally to different circumstances.

Emotion Myths and Facts

There are some common myths about emotions that are important to dispel:

Myth - Emotions just happen to us involuntarily.

Fact - While emotions are triggered automatically, we can influence emotions through our thoughts, beliefs, and behaviors.

Myth - Emotions are irrational and should not guide our actions.

Fact - Emotions contain data we can use wisely to respond adaptively, if we understand their underlying purposes.

Myth - Negative emotions are bad and should be suppressed.

Fact - All emotions provide useful information. The key is regulating emotions constructively.

Myth - Men and women feel emotions differently.

Fact - While influenced by gender roles, men and women experience the full range of human emotions.

Myth - Emotions are fleeting and disappear quickly.

Fact - Emotions can persist anywhere from minutes to days, requiring effective regulation.

Debunking misconceptions about emotions prevents maladaptive approaches like trying to ignore them or always following them blindly. The key is learning to view emotions with mindfulness and respond thoughtfully.

Individual Emotional Patterns

While all humans share core emotions, each person develops characteristic emotional patterns based on genetics, childhood experiences, role models, cognitive habits, and cultural factors. For instance, some patterns related to emotional reactivity include:

- **Intensity** - The strength of emotional reactions from mild to intense.
- **Frequency** - How often various emotions are felt from rarely to constantly.
- **Duration** - How long emotions persist before returning to baseline.
- **Latency** - How quickly emotions arise in response to triggers.
- **Threshold** - The intensity of triggers needed to provoke an emotional response.
- **Recovery** - The time needed to bounce back from emotional disturbances.

Other patterns relate to which emotions you experience more prominently or how emotions combine:

- **Predominant emotions** - The 2-3 emotions felt most frequently.
- **Emotion clusters** - Distinct combinations like anger + frustration or joy + calmness.
- **Emotion variability** - Fluctuations in emotions versus emotional stability.
- **Range of emotions** - The diversity of distinct emotions experienced.

By identifying your own engrained emotional patterns, you gain self-awareness to determine what you would like to change versus accept.

Investigating Your Emotional Patterns

To begin mapping your emotional landscape, set aside 30-60 minutes to complete the following questionnaire. Respond intuitively without overthinking.

Overall Emotional Landscape
- Would you describe your emotions as Mild, Moderate, or Intense?
- Are your emotions generally Constant, Occasional, or Rare?
- Do your emotions shift rapidly or persist for long periods?

Emotional Reactivity
- Does it take a Strong, Moderate, or Mild trigger for you to feel emotional?

- How quickly do you tend to react emotionally after a trigger?
- How long do your emotional reactions tend to last?
- How long does it take you to recover from strong emotions?

Emotional Range

- What are the 2-3 primary emotions you experience most frequently?
- Can you identify any consistent combinations or clusters of emotions unique to you?
- How much fluctuation do you experience in your emotions day to day?
- How many distinct emotions do you regularly feel? Do you experience emotions deeply?

Influential Factors

- What role models shaped your emotional habits growing up?
- How did your family express emotions? Were certain emotions unacceptable?
- How do you think culture/society impacts your emotions?
- Do you think genetics influence your emotional temperament?

Analyze your responses for insights. What did you learn about your emotional patterns? Which would you like to change? How could you leverage your natural patterns?

Emotion-Provoking Beliefs

Cognitive appraisal - your interpretations and beliefs about a situation - strongly influence which emotions you experience. The same event can spark entirely different emotions in two people based on their underlying beliefs.

For example, imagine your boss provides critical feedback on a project. You could interpret this feedback as:

- A sign your boss doesn't like you personally → Feelings of rejection
- Constructive advice to improve your skills → Feelings of determination
- An overwhelming personal failure → Feelings of humiliation
- A normal attempt to uphold standards → Feelings of acceptance

The emotion you feel - rejection, determination, humiliation, or acceptance - directly flows from your appraisal of the event.

In particular, look at the negative emotional appraisals above involving assumptions about your self-worth and abilities. These types of beliefs often underlie negative emotions like anxiety, anger, shame, and sadness.

Take a minute to reflect - when you feel strong unpleasant emotions, what core beliefs about yourself or the world are being activated?

Common Emotion-Provoking Beliefs

Here are some examples of beliefs that provoke difficult emotions:

- I am worthless or inadequate → Shame, sadness
- I am powerless → Fear, frustration

- I am unlovable → Rejection, jealousy
- The world is dangerous → Anxiety
- Others are hostile or abusive → Anger, disgust
- My needs don't matter → Anger, hurt
- I have no control → Helplessness
- I failed completely → Guilt
- I will be rejected or abandoned → Anxiety

Many emotional problems stem from distorted, irrational, or unhelpful beliefs about ourselves, others, and the world. The mind can catastrophize, exaggerate fears, minimize the positive, and jump to conclusions.

By uncovering the beliefs driving your emotions, you can reality test them against evidence and adopt alternative, empowering beliefs. This transforms how you appraise events and how you feel.

Activity: Identifying Your Emotion-Provoking Beliefs

Set a timer for 10 minutes. Quickly write down answers to the following questions:

- What beliefs or thoughts cross your mind when you feel anxious or worried?
- When you are sad or depressed what thoughts or interpretations reinforce this?
- What beliefs underly feelings of shame or embarrassment for you?
- What assumptions about yourself or others stir up anger in you?

- What interpretations make you feel rejected or hurt in relationships?
- How does your internal dialogue reinforce feelings of failure and guilt?

Look for patterns in the automatic thoughts and beliefs that may be distorting your emotions. Creating awareness of these beliefs is the first step to changing them.

Managing Emotion-Provoking Beliefs

Once you identify beliefs that provoke upsetting emotions, you can take steps to change this pattern:

- **Reality test** - How true and rational are the beliefs based on evidence? What alternative views exist?
- **Broaden perspective** - How might others perceive the situation differently? Am I overgeneralizing one instance?
- **Find exceptions** - When were there examples contradicting the belief?
- **Challenge distortions** - Am I exaggerating or catastrophizing without reason?
- **Consider contexts** - Are there contexts where the belief would not apply?
- **Adjust goals** - Do my beliefs stem from unrealistic expectations or perfectionism?
- **Affirm self-worth** - Remind yourself of your inherent value outside circumstances.
- **Adopt empowering beliefs** - Beliefs focused on growth, compassion, gratitude, and resilience.

With consistent effort, you can reshape habitual thought patterns. This puts you in control of your emotional experiences, instead of being controlled by dysfunctional beliefs.

The Mind-Emotion Connection

Your emotions and thoughts participate in a continual, bidirectional dance, influencing each other:

- **Thoughts → Emotions** – Appraisals and beliefs trigger emotions
- **Emotions → Thoughts** - Emotions focus thinking on concerns related to the feeling.
- **Thoughts → Emotions** - Analyzing emotions generates more thoughts about them.
- **Emotions → Thoughts** - Emotional states impact perception, memory, and interpretations.

For instance, feeling anxious may cause you to think more about potential threats, which reinforces the anxiety further. Feeling happy may trigger thoughts about your blessings, prolonging the happiness.

Since emotions and thoughts mutually impact each other, intervening at the thinking level can regulate emotions effectively. By changing emotion-provoking appraisals and beliefs, you alter emotional reactions.

Benefits of Emotional Awareness

Developing deep insight into your emotional patterns, beliefs, and experiences confers many advantages:

- Recognize unconscious influences on emotions like childhood programming.
- Identify destructive cognitive and behavioral habits.
- Notice consistent triggers for helpful versus unhelpful emotions.
- Prevent emotions from biasing thinking and decision making.
- Detect the early signs of rising emotions.
- Reality test initial appraisals of situations.
- Allow emotions without suppressing or overreacting to them.
- Select empowering beliefs that serve your growth and values.
- Understand your emotional needs and motivations.
- Communicate your inner states authentically to build intimacy.

In short, emotional awareness is the bedrock for constructing emotional intelligence skills. It puts you in the driver's seat, instead of emotions controlling your actions unconsciously.

Chapter 1 - Key Points

- Emotions evolved as adaptive signals to survive threats and seize opportunities.
- Your emotional experiences contain multiple components including appraisals, physical sensations, and action urges.
- All humans share a set of basic, primary emotions like joy, anger, fear, disgust, sadness.
- Each person develops characteristic emotional patterns based on life experiences and genetics.

- The beliefs you hold about situations strongly shape your emotional reactions to them.
- Developing insight into your emotional patterns and beliefs allows you to regulate your emotions consciously.

Chapter 1 - Reflection Question

What are 1-2 key insights you gained about your personal emotional patterns or beliefs? How will these shape your EQ journey going forward?

Chapter 2: Mastering Emotion Regulation

In chapter 1, we explored the nature of emotions and patterns in your emotional landscape. Now it's time to build the crucial capacity to regulate your emotions constructively.

Emotion regulation means intentionally influencing your emotional experiences and expressions to respond adaptively to situations. Instead of being swept away by intense emotions, you can learn to manage your feelings effectively.

The Costs of Poor Emotion Regulation

We all face emotions we wish we didn't feel. But those who lack strategies to modulate their emotions often suffer consequences:

- Reacting impulsively based on anger, hurt, or anxiety
- Making poor decisions in the heat of emotion
- Ruining relationships with emotional outbursts
- Sinking into depressive, guilty, or fearful states
- Resorting to harmful strategies for dealing with difficulties, such as relying on substances for relief.
- Feeling emotionally exhausted
- Losing motivation after setbacks

Emotions amplified out of control can damage your relationships, derail your plans, and sabotage your well-being. Learning emotion regulation gives you the power to handle disruptive emotions gracefully.

The Emotional Mind vs. Rational Mind

"When you are raging mad, you often can't think straight." - Daniel Goleman

To understand why we lose control of emotions, it helps to view the mind as having two distinct modes:

> **Emotional Mind** - This reactive mode operates automatically based on emotions, impulses, and associations. It is fast, instinctive, and often irrational.

> **Rational Mind** - This mode thinks deliberatively through logic, evidence, and reasoning. It is slower, reflective, and more rational.

You need both modes to function optimally. The emotional mind identifies urgent concerns for the rational mind to analyze and resolve. Problems arise when the emotional mind overwhelms your rational thinking.

For example, when you feel intense anger, your rational mind gets hijacked by emotional impulses to lash out or make accusations you later regret. Or when you are terrified, emotion narrows your focus to run away immediately rather than considering options.

Learning to apply your rational mind to balance and broaden the emotional mind is key for mastery. This enables you to respond thoughtfully according to your values, instead of being a slave to each passing emotion.

Observe Your Emotional Mind

Start developing awareness of your emotional mind by doing this quick meditation:

Set a timer for one minute. Close your eyes and focus solely on your breathing without trying to alter it. If thoughts arise, gently return your attention to the breath.

After one minute, answer these questions:

- Were you able to maintain focus on the breath?
- What kinds of thoughts arose?
- How did your body feel?
- What emotions arose mildly?

This meditation provides a micro-glimpse into the automatic workings of your emotional mind. The mental chatter and associations reflect your subconscious patterns.

With practice extending this meditation, you gain greater insight into how emotions, thoughts, and bodily feelings operate together in your emotional mind. This awareness alone starts diluting their intensity.

Create an Emotion Action Plan

The time to take control of your emotions is _before_ you feel overwhelmed by them. By planning ahead, you can respond wisely in challenging situations.

Follow these steps to create your own Emotion Action Plan:

Step 1 - Choose a recurrent negative emotion like anxiety, anger, or sadness.

Step 2 - Dissect what happens when you feel this emotion. What thoughts arise? How does your body react? What action urges do you experience?

Step 3 - Consider past situations where this emotion caused problems. What lessons can you draw?

Step 4 - Brainstorm rational responses. What thoughts could bring perspective? What actions align with your values?

Step 5 - Draft an if-then plan. IF the emotion arises, THEN I will take these rational steps:

When I feel [emotion], I will:
1. [Thought strategy]
2. [Thought strategy]
3. [Action strategy]
4. [Action strategy]

Having a plan empowers you to channel emotions wisely. Rehearse it mentally to build readiness. With practice, this gives your rational mind control.

Defuse from Intense Emotions

When you find yourself in the grip of intense emotion, use these steps to activate your rational mind:

1. **Take a time out** - Give yourself space by leaving the situation temporarily. This allows emotions to cool down naturally.
2. **Breathe consciously** - Rhythmic, deep breathing turns on your parasympathetic nervous system to counter fight-or-flight arousal.
3. **Get in touch with sensations**** - Scan your body and notice any tension or discomfort. Relax these areas.
4. **Observe thoughts non-judgmentally** - Instead of getting swept up in the emotional storyline, watch thoughts pass by impartially.

5. **Ask what is underneath the emotion** - Dig beneath the surface feeling. What core need or belief is triggering this?
6. **Speak to yourself compassionately** - What would you say to comfort a friend feeling this way? Offer yourself similar empathy.
7. **Broaden perspective** - Consider the bigger picture, context, and your core values. How else can you view the situation?
8. **Make rational decisions** - Now that you have regained composure, reassess how to respond adaptively.

Defusion techniques allow intense emotions to naturally subside so your wise mind can guide responses, not your emotional mind.

Change Negative Emotional Habits

Many emotional problems originate from habitual patterns engraved in your brain. The good news is the brain stays malleable - you can literally reshape emotional circuits through practice.

Identify a negative emotional habit you want to curb like anger, anxiety, or constant worrying. Then design a practice to rewire this pattern:

- **Choose a trigger event** - A situation that predictably sparks the unwanted emotion.
- **Prepare a new response** - How could you respond differently using the techniques in this chapter? Rehearse it mentally.

- **Put yourself in the trigger situation** - Gradually expose yourself to the event in a controlled way.
- **Practice your new response** - When you notice the emotion arising, consciously implement your planned response.
- **Reward yourself** - Celebrate acting intentionally rather than reactively.
- **Repeat consistently** - Frequent practice strengthens and automates the new neural pathway.

With commitment, you can master emotions that used to control you through intentional practice. Your brain will adapt.

Strategies to Regulate Difficult Emotions

Here are effective strategies to apply your rational mind to regulate unhelpful emotions:

For anxiety:
- Identify worst case scenarios and make contingency plans.
- Challenge anxious assumptions by collecting counterevidence.
- Shift focus to the present moment using grounding techniques.
- Practice tolerating uncertainty without needing constant reassurance.
- Visualize handling challenges successfully.

For sadness:

- Let yourself feel sadness fully, without wallowing in it.
- Identify lessons learned and meaning gained through the loss.
- Focus on one step at a time rather than overwhelming big picture changes.
- Imagine how your future self will feel looking back with more perspective.
- List current reasons to feel grateful, not defined solely by loss.

For anger:
- Consider if misinterpreting motivations or making assumptions about others' behavior.
- Communicate anger assertively rather than aggressively. Use "I feel __" statements.
- Write in a journal to process anger and hurt underneath it.
- Release anger through vigorous exercise, punching bags, screaming in the car.
- Set boundaries directly rather than bottling up resentment.

For guilt:
- Apologize for impacts of your actions without condemning your core self.
- Make amends through improved behavior going forward.
- Grant yourself forgiveness for your humanity and the errors you've made.
- Consider lessons learned that will lead to better choices next time.

- Imagine forgiving a friend struggling with similar guilt. Extend that compassion to yourself.

Tailor strategies to target your specific emotional challenges. The more options you have, the more agile you become at regulating emotions as needed in the moment.

Developing Emotional Agility

Emotional agility means adapting your responses fluidly to meet the needs of any situation. To have this agility, Columbia psychologist Elke Van Hoof identifies three skills:

1. **Accepting discomfort** - Feeling emotions without being controlled by them. Rather than avoiding pain or becoming overwhelmed, you remain present.
2. **Seeing situations clearly** - Observing experiences accurately, without the bias of your emotional state distorting perceptions.
3. **Acting according to values** - Choosing wise responses, beyond knee-jerk emotional reactions, that serve your highest intentions.

While acceptance provides the foundation, flexibility stems from toggling deliberately between the emotional mind and rational mind. You remain anchored yet responsive.

When you integrate these skills, you can turn life's obstacles into opportunities for growth instead of being paralyzed by difficult emotions. You become CEO of your inner world.

Turning Emotional Pain into Insight

"Suffering ceases to be suffering when it has meaning." - Viktor Frankl

When faced with emotional pain, avoid trying to simply shut it down. Instead, investigate it for the wisdom and insight it contains:

Ask probing questions:
- What is hurting or threatened that I must acknowledge?
- How is this emotion trying to help me by signaling important needs?
- What limiting beliefs is this bringing to my attention?
- How can I learn from this to make better choices going forward?

Extract the lessons:
- What improvements do I need to make?
- How can I avoid similar pitfalls in the future?
- What am I now motivated and equipped to change?
- What new priorities or boundaries would serve me?

See the benefits:
- How did this experience help me grow?
- What inner strengths did this reveal that I can rely on?
- How did this shed light on my values to guide me?
- What empathy and wisdom have I gained to share with others?

Extracting meaning transforms emotions that once weighed you down into rocket fuel propelling your growth.

Chapter 2 - Key Points

- Emotion regulation means influencing what emotions you have, when, and how you experience or express them.
- Poor emotion regulation results in impulsive reactions, mental overwhelm, strained relationships, and unhealthy coping behaviors.
- The emotional mind can hijack rational thinking when we become flooded with intense feelings.
- Defusion techniques like breath focus, body scanning, and thought watching can calm the emotional storm so reasoning can prevail.
- You can rewrite longstanding emotional habits through intentional practice responding differently.
- Emotional agility comes from toggling fluidly between your emotional mind and rational mind.
- Difficult emotions contain vital insights - lean into the pain to extract the wisdom for growth.

Chapter 2 - Reflection Question

- What are 1-2 emotion regulation strategies you can start applying today? How will mastering your emotions more consciously change your life?

Chapter 3: Motivation Through Emotional Wisdom

The previous chapters focused on building emotional awareness and regulation. Now we build the bridge from self-management to using emotions wisely to drive motivation and achievement.

Motivation fueled by emotional wisdom provides the power to persevere when external rewards and validation disappear. By tapping into purpose and meaning, you gain an internal compass to guide your life's journey.

Fleeting Happiness From External Rewards

Many people spend their lives chasing happiness through external rewards like money, status, fame, possessions, physical appearance, or pleasing others. But research reveals this happiness quickly fades:

- The thrill of buying your dream home diminishes as you adjust to it.
- The euphoria after a promotion or raise wears off.
- New cars lose their luster once they become your regular vehicle.
- Vacations provide temporary relief from daily stresses.

These rewards provide joy in the moment, but it is temporary since your mind adapts to your new circumstances. This "hedonic adaptation" means you always need more to keep chasing the happiness high.

This differs from sustainable happiness cultivated from within. While external successes may accompany internal fulfillment, they are inherently unreliable sources of lasting motivation and satisfaction.

The Hedonic Treadmill of Material Success

Psychologist Sonja Lyubomirsky uses the metaphor of a treadmill to describe how people end up running faster chasing external rewards, just to stay in the same place happiness-wise:

- You strive to earn more income, thinking it will make you happy. But your lifestyle expands, and you fall into comparing yourself to those with even greater wealth.
- You amplify your social media following, expecting it to boost your morale. But you become addicted to external validation through likes and comments.
- You purchase a luxury car, anticipating feelings of pride and accomplishment. But within months you barely notice the car's beauty as it becomes your new normal.
- You get accepted to your dream university. But soon social and academic pressures consume you, minimizing any sense of achievement.

The treadmill can apply to relationships as well. People idealize a perfect partner who will complete them, only to grapple with the same internal struggles.

Getting off the treadmill requires looking inward to define success and fulfillment for yourself. This provides stable psychological ground to build resilience.

Sources of Internal Motivation

Lasting motivation comes from internal sources, not external. Here are key sources of internal drive and inspiration:

Values

Your values reflect what matters most - how you aspire to treat yourself and others. They invoke a deep sense of purpose. Identify 5-10 core values like learning, creativity, honesty, courage, generosity, and persistence. Choose values that energize you emotionally and align with your best self.

Vision

A life vision paints a vivid mental image of the person you aspire to become and the world you aim to create. It energizes you to manifest this ideal future. Describe your vision through essentials like fulfilling relationships, personal growth, desired feelings, and contributions.

Purpose

Your purpose involves the unique skills and passions you bring that improve the world in special ways only you can. Discover this by analyzing your innate strengths and experiences. What issues call you into service? How can you help others along their journeys?

Goals

Once you have defined larger purpose and vision, set specific, measurable goals to work toward them. Whether improving your health, advancing your career, or building a company, go after life-enriching goals bigger than yourself.

Mindset
Adopt empowering beliefs about challenges, change, willpower, confidence, and resilience. Condition your mindset through affirmations, visualization, and identifying limiting thought patterns. Your mindset provides the mental fuel.

Tapping these internal sources provides renewable motivation. When you know your deepest values, all choices become clearer. You become the master of your fate.

Turning Happiness Into a Life Force

The Dalai Lama distinguishes two forms of happiness:
- **Happiness Dependent on External Conditions** - This fleeting happiness relies on acquiring objects, success, good fortune, or approval of others. It is inherently unstable.
- **Unconditional Happiness** - This form arises from intentionally cultivating wisdom, inner peace, and altruism. It is more reliable since it cannot be taken away.

The first form still has worth - appreciating life's temporary joys and pleasures nurtures well-being. But long-term fulfillment requires generating happiness from within, as the second form describes.

Consider times you felt incredible bliss, meaning, or inspiration. Likely these arose from sources like:

- Helping someone in need
- Expressing gratitude
- Feeling totally present
- Using your strengths
- Sharing laughter and joy
- Bonding deeply with others
- Achieving a challenging goal
- Understanding yourself profoundly
- Contributing to something larger than yourself

These experiences illuminate your inner light. Your task is to integrate activities eliciting these states into your daily routines. Soon you generate happiness naturally wherever you go.

Design a Life That Fills Your Spirit

Essentialism author Greg McKeown offers a framework for living meaningfully he calls CANEI:

C - **Contribution** - How do you make a difference and serve others?

A - **Accomplishment** - What gives you a sense of achievement and pride?

N - **Nourishment** - What activities replenish your mental, physical, emotional, and spiritual health?

E - **Ease** - Where do you find fun, joy, and stress relief?

I - **Influence** - How do you persuade and support others' dreams?

Take an hour to brainstorm how you currently (or wish to) incorporate each element. For example:

Contribution - volunteering, mentoring others

Accomplishment - completing key projects, learning new skills

Nourishment - cooking healthy foods, reading, spending time in nature

Ease - socializing with friends, listening to music, enjoying hobbies

Influence - parenting children, motivating those around you

Look for gaps where you need more balance. Revise routines to better align with your motivational needs.

Motivation From Flow States

Flow states occur when you feel completely absorbed in focused, meaningful challenges that match your abilities. First identified by psychologist Mihaly Csikszentmihalyi, characteristics include:

- Intense focus and involvement
- Merging of action and awareness
- Loss of self-consciousness
- Feeling control over the situation
- Distortion of time perception
- Finding inherent satisfaction in engaging in the activity.

Athletes call it *"being in the zone."* Musicians describe it as rhythm taking over. Flow states motivate by providing profound enjoyment from applying your gifts passionately.

You likely experience flow when playing sports, creating art, playing instruments, gardening, cooking, reading, writing, and engaging other hobbies. Flow arises from the sweet spot between boredom (under-challenged) and anxiety (over-challenged).

By identifying your flow triggers, you can structure more time for these re-energizing passions. Set goals just beyond your comfort zone to stretch your abilities. Becoming immersed in endeavors you love will motivate you to keep growing.

Actualizing Your Hierarchy of Needs

Psychologist Abraham Maslow's Hierarchy of Needs reveals that people must satisfy lower needs before focusing on higher psychological needs related to growth:

> **Self-actualization** - Achieving full potential
> **Esteem** - Confidence, respect, recognition
> **Love/belonging** - Relationships, intimacy
> **Safety** - Security, routine
> **Physiological** - Food, water, shelter

Thriving people make self-actualization their life goal. But it's easier to actualize your potential after securing safety, belonging, esteem and having vital physical needs met.

Assess where you feel potential deficits lower on the pyramid that drain you. Are you struggling for money or housing? Feeling lonely or disconnected? Do you lack self-confidence and respect? Healing these areas provides the foundation to pursue meaningful self-actualization.

On the other hand, people with ample resources and relationships may still feel empty inside. Self-actualization requires defining your unique purpose and fully applying your gift to it. Recognize that a rich life – filled with learning, compassion and purpose - is available right now.

Live Your Eulogy Today

Motivation depends on regularly revisiting the big picture. The most powerful frame is imagining your life reflections as you reach old age:

- What memories and accomplishments will you look back on proudly?
- What qualities and values do you want people to appreciate about you?
- What positive impacts will you have made on your family, community, the world?
- How do you hope people describe your influence on them?
- What adventures, challenges, joys, and wisdom will fill your soul with fulfillment?

Essentially, imagine the eulogy you hope loved ones will share at your funeral - then make choices today to live up to this vision. When struggling with direction, ask if your current path aligns with the eulogy you desire.

You only get one life - make choices motivated by how you wish to be remembered in the end. Never settle for less than your highest vision for yourself.

Chapter 3 - Key Points

- Motivation fueled by external rewards like money, status, and praise fades as you adapt to having those needs met.

- Lasting motivation stems from discovering your core values and aligning actions with your life's purpose and vision.
- Choose work, relationships, and hobbies that help you enter flow states - feeling fully engaged and challenged.
- Fulfillment ultimately comes from actualizing your full potential and living your eulogy today.
- Build unconditional happiness through serving others, using your strengths, feeling present, and nourishing your whole being.

Chapter 3 - Reflection Question

- How can you structure more motivation and fulfillment into your daily life based on what gives you meaning?

Chapter 4: The Path to Empathy

We have explored building emotional intelligence intrapersonally - from self-awareness to motivation. Now we connect emotional skills outwards through the bridge of empathy.

Empathy means recognizing emotions in others, understanding their perspective, and connecting with compassion. This social-emotional capacity enriches all your relationships.

This chapter provides research and exercises to help you walk in others' shoes, communicate empathetically, and deepen bonds through vulnerability and listening.

What is Empathy?

Empathy involves three key abilities according to psychologist Daniel Goleman:

1. **Cognitive Empathy** - Understanding someone's perspective by imagining yourself in their position.
2. **Emotional Empathy** - Feeling what someone else feels by mirroring their emotions.
3. **Empathic Concern** - Using empathy to tune into someone's needs and offer support.

Cognitive empathy helps you grasp how events impact others based on their experiences. Emotional empathy creates resonance with their feelings. Combining both allows you to transmit compassion.

The Evolutionary Roots of Empathy

Empathy has evolutionary roots in attachment bonding between parents and offspring. When a child cried, empathic parents mirrored the distress, motivating them to soothe their baby. This nurturing contributed to survival.

In adults, empathy facilitates social cohesion. By picking up on emotional cues, you can adapt behavior compassionately, preventing conflict and abandonment from others. Psychologist Martin Hoffman describes how empathy develops:

1. **Mimicry** - As infants, we automatically mimic faces, sounds, and movements, causing us to converge emotionally.
2. **Classical Conditioning** - We associate other's emotions with our own past feelings in similar contexts, priming empathy.
3. **Direct Association** - We learn that other's inner states cause their expressions and behaviors, allowing reverse inference.
4. **Perspective-taking** - As cognitive abilities mature, we can imagine different viewpoints to understand varied reactions.
5. **Verbal Mediation**- Language provides shared symbols to describe internal states, facilitating empathy through communication.

In summary, empathy has innate and learned aspects. We are primed to emotionally converge with others, but perspective-taking ultimately makes empathy possible.

Obstacles to Empathy

Despite inborn empathy circuits, limitations and biases can inhibit empathy:

- **Emotional overload** - When feeling distressed yourself, it's harder to empathize until you self-soothe.
- **Threat response** - Social conditioning causes some to see different groups or personalities as threats, blocking empathy.
- **In-group bias** - It's easier to empathize with those you identify with, making it harder to empathize with "outsiders."
- **Impact bias** - People underestimate their ability to adapt to adverse events, so they under-empathize with others' resilience.
- **Egocentrism** - Focusing attention inward can lead to forgetting other viewpoints exist outside your own experience.
- **Conformity bias** - When others do not express empathy, failing to perceive social cues, people follow the crowd.

Recognizing these roadblocks helps you proactively choose empathy, even when difficult. You can relate to all people - whether allies, opponents, or strangers - through shared humanity.

Benefits of Empathy

Beyond aiding cooperation, modern research reveals numerous benefits of empathy:

- **Physical health** – Empathy lowers stress by calming the threat response to people perceived different or hostile. It also reduces anxiety by making the world seem safer through human connection.
- **Relationships** – Empathy builds trust, intimacy, and effective communication. It prevents conflicts from escalating by promoting peaceful understanding.
- **Courage** – Seeing life through others' realities expands your worldview. This gives you the courage to connect across differences.
- **Morality** – Empathy drives moral action by causing you to care about how your choices impact others. It underlies kindness, charity, and justice.
- **Self-compassion** – Practicing empathy for yourself combats destructive self-criticism. It allows accepting imperfections as part of the shared human experience.
- **Leadership** – Leaders who relate to followers' needs and struggles unify and inspire people. Empathy makes leadership emotionally compelling.

You can enrich every area of life by cultivating empathy. It provides insight into the richness behind all human behavior.

Active Listening Techniques

One key way to demonstrate empathy is through active listening. When someone is speaking to you, use these skills:

- **Give your full attention** - Avoid distractions and make regular eye contact to show you are engaged.

- **Withhold judgments** - Let them finish before forming conclusions. Avoid thinking ahead to your desired response.
- **Reflect back content** - Paraphrase key points to show your understanding. Ask clarifying questions.
- **Reflect back feelings** - Note emotional aspects like "You seem discouraged." Make sure to have read the person accurately.
- **Express support** - Show you are on their side through reassuring words and body language.
- **Ask exploratory questions** - Inquire to learn more without interrogation. "What made that such a challenge for you?"
- **Suspend advice** - Often people just need to feel heard. Give advice only if explicitly asked.

Convey presence through patience, acceptance, and using the person's language. They should feel safe opening up to you.

Vulnerability Builds Bonds

Brené Brown's research discovered that the key trait of those with a strong sense of love and belonging is vulnerability. Being open about imperfections paradoxically helps others relate to and accept you.

She defines vulnerability as "uncertainty, risk, and emotional exposure." While this feels counterintuitive, here are some examples of how vulnerability nurtures intimacy in relationships:

- Admitting a mistake shows you are human, not perfect.
- Sharing an insecurity displays trust in the other person.

- Seeking advice demonstrates respect for their wisdom.
- Expressing emotion authentically bonds you through shared humanity.
- Asking for help when struggling avoids superficial interactions.

Of course, you want to share vulnerably in appropriate contexts, just as others open up gradually in return. But having the courage to let down masks builds reciprocal care and understanding.

Empathic Concern In Difficult Situations

Even in conflict, you can access empathy to de-escalate and find common ground. Consider two examples:

- **A friend constantly complains but rejects solutions** - Rather than shutting her down, recognize she needs catharsis. You can empathize how difficult her problems feel while upholding boundaries about what support works for you.
- **A family member makes hurtful remarks** - Before retaliating, try to understand their motivations and insecurities fueling the behavior. Perhaps they avoid vulnerable feelings by lashing out. Compassion opens doors.

Of course, you must protect against emotional or physical harm too. But empathy gives you power to transform difficult situations and facilitate mutual growth.

Comforting Others

When someone comes to you distressed, empathy allows you to provide comfort effectively:

- First, offer an empathetic **emotional label** like "*You seem really sad.*" Make sure you read their emotions accurately.
- Share a **personal example** when you felt a similar emotion to convey understanding.
- Identify the likely **core need** driving their feelings. "*It sounds like you are needing more security in your relationship right now.*"
- Offer **hope and reassurance** to build resilience. "I know this is so painful right now, but I truly believe things will get better in time."
- Brainstorm **potential solutions** they could try to improve the situation. Provide recommendations if requested.
- Simply **be present** through emotional support and practical help. Follow their lead on what they need most.

You do not actually need to solve people's problems. Empathy shows you comprehend their experience, which paradoxically helps them handle challenges.

The Empathetic Mindset

Here are core principles to integrate to develop an empathetic mindset:

- See life through others' perspectives, not just your own.
- Assume people have valid reasons for their emotions and behaviors.
- Suspend judgment; avoid assumptions about people's motivations or character.

- Embrace shared human vulnerability rather than viewing yourself as essentially different.
- Relate to people's core humanity rather than surface level identities and beliefs.
- Approach all interactions with compassion for people's innate worth and desire for happiness like your own.

Empathy takes daily practice and vigilance to overcome automatic egocentrism. But it offers the reward of relationships built on care, trust, and positive influence.

Develop Cognitive Empathy Through Reading

An impactful way to build cognitive empathy is by reading diverse literature exposing you to varied life experiences. Good options include:

- **Memoirs** - Learn how major events impacted real people through their personal accounts.
- **Historical fiction** - Walk in the shoes of someone from a different country or time period.
- **Literary fiction** - Experience what it is like to grapple with universal life challenges.
- **Poetry/Essays** - Gain insight into authors' inner worlds and social commentary.
- **Ethnographies** - Study an unfamiliar community or culture from their point of view.
- **Biographies** - Understand public figures' motivations, dreams, and roadblocks.

Immerse yourself in in-depth stories about protagonists who have different backgrounds and beliefs from yourself. This stretches your circle of empathy.

Loving-Kindness Meditation

This meditation exercise builds empathy by consciously directing caring feelings outward:

1. Sit comfortably, close your eyes, and relax your muscles. Take a few deep breaths.
2. Call to mind someone you care about like a close friend or family member. Picture them and their good qualities.
3. Silently wish them well. "May you be happy. May you be healthy. May you be safe from harm." Send them love.
4. Expand your awareness to include other people you appreciate and wish well, connecting to their fundamental humanity.
5. Widen this compassion to include neutral people you encounter like neighbors, then difficult people who stir negative emotions. Wish all beings well.
6. Finally, include yourself. "May I be happy. May I be healthy. May I live with ease." Bathe in this loving feeling.

Practice loving-kindness meditation regularly to cultivate an open heart. It builds bonds of empathy that extend ever wider.

Chapter 4 - Key Points

- Empathy requires understanding perspectives (cognitive empathy), connecting emotionally (emotional empathy), and acting with compassion.

- Despite having an innate capacity for empathy, biases can inhibit our openness to differing experiences.
- Active listening, expressing vulnerability, comforting others, and reading diverse literature expands empathy.
- A steady practice of loving-kindness meditation instills empathy toward all people, including oneself.
- Empathy enables you to have courageous conversations, de-escalate conflict, support others, and build intimacy.

Chapter 4 - Reflection Question
- What relationships or conflicts in your life would improve through greater empathy? How can you cultivate an empathetic mindset?

Chapter 5: Apply Emotional Intelligence Outward

We have built a strong foundation of self-awareness, self-management, empathy, and motivation fueled by meaning. Now it is time to apply emotional intelligence skills to enrich your relationships and leadership.

This chapter shares techniques to communicate effectively, offer compassionate feedback, navigate conflict gracefully, and influence people from an emotionally wise place.

Emotional Intelligence Creates Effective Communication

Communication pervades life, yet few practice it skillfully. Emotional intelligence helps you converse with others in ways that build trust and understanding. Follow these principles:

1. **Attune to the other person** - Notice their emotion state, mood, verbal and nonverbal cues. Do not force topics that do not resonate given their mindset.

2. **Express your message congruently** - Ensure your words, tone, and body language align. Incongruence undermines trustworthiness.

3. **Speak assertively, not aggressively** - State your perspectives, needs, and boundaries while respecting others. Leave room for collaborative problem solving.

4. **Be descriptive, not evaluative** - Describe situations factually and own your interpretations. Avoid judgments about other's character or motivations.

5. **Listen deeply**- Reflect back content and feelings. Make the other person feel heard and valued. Suspend defensiveness.
6. **Find common ground** - Identify shared goals and values to nurture mutual understanding, even amidst disagreement.
7. **Take responsibility for your role** - Apologize for any insensitive actions without blaming. Model openness to feedback.
8. **Problem solve collaboratively** - Brainstorm solutions that allow mutual needs to be met. Compromise where necessary.

Let these principles guide challenging conversations. Your emotional maturity can positively influence relationships.

Providing Constructive Feedback

Offering sensitive feedback when someone needs to improve requires strong emotional skills. Follow these steps:

1. **Time it thoughtfully** - Choose an appropriate setting when the person is receptive. Don't criticize in front of others.
2. **Frame positively** - Note their strengths first. Provide reassuring context that you believe in their abilities.
3. **Describe the problem behavior specifically** - Avoid vague or exaggerated complaints. Stick to factual examples.
4. **Explain effects non-judgmentally** - Note how the behavior affects you and others without blame or assumptions.

5. **Invite their perspectives** - There may be valid reasons or mitigating circumstances behind their actions. Seek to understand.

6. **Brainstorm solutions together** - Ask how they would suggest improving. Collaborate on an action plan you both agree to.

7. **Express care** - Convey sincere appreciation for them and confidence they will succeed with adaptations.

With thoughtful communication, you can provide constructive feedback that motivates change without provoking defensiveness.

Managing Interpersonal Conflict

Conflicts inevitably arise in relationships when needs clash. Handled poorly, resentments linger. But approached skillfully, conflicts present opportunities for deeper connection through mutual understanding.

Apply these conflict resolution steps:

- **Listen first** - Allow the upset person to express themselves fully before defending yourself.

- **Find common interests** - Agree on shared relationship goals and values not currently being met.

- **Take responsibility** - Sincerely apologize for your role without deflecting blame onto the other.

- **Explain your needs non-judgmentally** - Use "I feel __" statements about your expectations. Avoid criticism.

- **Generate solutions** - Brainstorm ways for both parties' needs to be satisfied. Identify workable compromises.

- **Implement and follow up** - Clarify next steps and schedule future conversations to track progress.
- **Forgive** - Make the intentional choice to release resentment and re-commit to mutual care and trust.

Holding a loving mindset focused on win-win collaborative solutions defuses arguments. You transform conflicts into bonding experiences.

Cultivating Influence and Inspiration

Great leaders succeed not through formal authority alone - they influence people by connecting emotionally. Research shows leaders who develop the following six abilities inspire others to follow them:

- **Self-awareness** - They know their own values, principles, emotions, strengths, and weaknesses.
- **Self-regulation** - They manage their reactions skillfully even under stress and adversity.
- **Motivation** - They feel driven by intrinsic passion for their work and care for their people.
- **Empathy** - They understand people's diverse perspectives, needs, hopes, and fears.
- **Social skills** - They build rapport, resolve conflicts, and facilitate cooperation.
- **Vision** - They articulate a compelling vision of the future that energizes people.

Essentially, leadership stems from your inner world. By growing self-knowledge and emotional wisdom, you gain confidence and social capital. Your integrity and compassion mobilize people to work toward common aims.

Emotional Intelligence Creates Compelling Stories

Stories stir people profoundly by making ideas emotionally resonant. When communicating values or vision, weave in purposeful narratives:

- **Share your journey** - Make concepts tangible by articulating how they impacted you personally. People invest in leaders committed for the right reasons.
- **Spotlight individuals** - Help exemplars and their growth come alive. This makes ideals feel accessible.
- **Describe key moments** - Turn points that shifted perspective provide drama and revelation.
- **Use vivid imagery** - Visual details like metaphors stick in memory by engaging imagination along with intellect.
- **Structure as a hero's journey** - Emphasize rising to meet challenges and undergoing transformation.
- **Appeal to shared dreams and fears** - Tap into common hopes and struggles to create connection.
- **Build to a purposeful ending** - Share lessons learned to inspire others toward growth and action.

Stir hearts as well as minds. Masterful storytelling makes leadership emotionally compelling. Values take on flesh and blood.

Complementing Success and Sacrifice

As a leader aiming to motivate people, understand that highlighting achievements has an opposite side:

Praising accomplishments addresses the **promise** - the hopeful vision people work toward. But you must also acknowledge the **price** - the sacrifices, doubts, and trials overcome chasing the vision.

Celebrating accomplishments motivates by showing what is possible. But unless you empathize with the pain behind progress, people feel unable to relate.

Strike the right balance when sharing stories:

- Note the preparation and strategic choices that led to success.
- Share raw glimpses of the setbacks faced and emotional resilience required.
- Emphasize *"We"* - how people supported each other through mutual sacrifice.
- Inspire with purpose greater than oneself that makes trials worthwhile.
- Encourage people that if these exemplars can rise up, they can too.

People give their all when they comprehend the cost and recognize their own struggles in those who achieved greatness.

Chapter 5 - Key Points

- Emotional attunement, assertive communication, and collaborative conflict resolution preserve relationships.
- Feedback is best received when delivered thoughtfully and framed constructively.
- Addressing conflicts directly as win-win situations deepens mutual understanding.
- Influence stems from self-knowledge, integrity, care for people, and articulating purpose.

- Stir people's hearts through storytelling that highlights transformation and service of shared ideals.

Chapter 5 - Reflection Question

- What scenarios can you practice applying these relationship management skills toward - whether at home, work, or in your community?

Chapter 6: Your Emotional Intelligence Journey

We have now explored the full terrain of emotional intelligence - from building self-awareness to applying emotional skills in relationships and leadership. In this final chapter, we will review key lessons, tools, and practices to carry forward. I will also provide guidance to continue advancing your EQ over a lifetime.

Pathway to Mastery

Let's briefly revisit the roadmap that structures this book:

- **Chapter 1** introduced core concepts like the evolutionary purpose of emotions, components of emotional experiences, and your personal patterns.
- **Chapter 2** covered emotion regulation techniques to manage disruptive emotional habits and defuse from distress.
- **Chapter 3** discussed deriving motivational fuel from your values, flow states, and service to purpose.
- **Chapter 4** explained empathy's importance for courageous relationships and methods to grow perspective-taking.
- **Chapter 5** highlighted applying EQ to communication, conflict resolution, leadership influence, and storytelling.

While we only scratched the surface of each area, you now possess a powerful framework, toolset, and practices to continue developing your emotional intelligence.

Internalizing Key Emotional Skills

Here are 10 essential emotional intelligence skills to review and integrate into your daily life:

1. **Recognize patterns** - Monitor your characteristic emotional reactions, habits, and biases.
2. **Name emotions** - Label feelings in the moment to manage them effectively.
3. **Accept all emotions** - Let yourself feel without suppressing or overindulging emotions.
4. **Defuse from distress** - Shift attention to gain rational distance from overwhelming emotions.
5. **Reality test interpretations** - Consider alternative appraisals of triggering situations.
6. **Change self-defeating beliefs** - Replace distorted thought patterns with more accurate beliefs about yourself, others, and the world.
7. **Communicate needs constructively** - Use "I feel __" statements to take ownership of your experience.
8. **Set boundaries skillfully** - Clarity around what treatment you expect creates stable relationships.
9. **Repair conflicts** - Focus on understanding others' valid perspectives instead of defending your ego.
10. **Take responsible action** - Align behavior with your values rather than acting impulsively.

Which of these skills resonate most as abilities you need to continue honing? Deliberately practice them.

Daily Tools to Develop EQ

Here are exercises you can incorporate into your daily routine to sustain emotional growth:

- **Morning ritual** - Set a positive tone by writing down 3-5 things you feel grateful for. Visualize compassion extending from your heart outwards.
- **Check-in questions** - During transitions in the day, pause to ask "What emotions am I feeling right now?" "How are these emotions serving me?" "How can I respond thoughtfully?"
- **Mindful transitions** - Find small opportunities like walking, washing dishes, or brushing your teeth to anchor attention on bodily sensations. This expands self-awareness.
- **Reflective journaling** - Free write about emotions you felt that day, what you learned about yourself, how to approach ongoing challenges etc. Process experiences.
- **Loving-kindness meditation** - Take 5-10 minutes each day to send care and good wishes outward to loved ones, neutral people, those suffering, and yourself.
- **Relaxation practice** - Wind down by listening to calming music, enjoying a hot bath, or doing gentle stretches. Manage your nervous system.
- **Peer support** - Share joys, trials, and lessons with trusted friends who can offer empathy and alternative perspectives.
- **Read literature** - Fiction expands emotional awareness and cognitive empathy by immersing you in diverse characters' internal worlds.

- **Savor experiences** - Deliberately appreciate each experience - a walk, conversation, meal, etc. Infuse daily life with meaning.
- **Keep growing** - Continue exploring EQ by reading, attending workshops, or taking courses. Never stop learning.

Weave small practices into the fabric of your days to steady emotional progress. Plan which you will begin this week!

Long-Term EQ Goals to Set

While daily practices build emotional muscle memory, you also want to set larger goals to stretch your capacities over years. Reflect on a few 1-3 year EQ goals. Some ideas:

- Meet regularly with a peer support group to discuss growth.
- Volunteer weekly with an organization helping those in need to build empathy and meaning.
- Write a book, blog, or speakers share your lessons learned to guide others.
- Take an intensive course on nonviolent communication, counseling, or leadership psychology.
- Participate in a meditation or EQ retreat to deepen self-knowledge.
- Engage a coach to tailor EQ practices for your psychology and ambitions.
- Travel to learn from other cultures developing emotional and social intelligence.
- Take up arts like music, pottery, poetry, or painting for self-discovery and flow.

- Attend counseling to work through deep-seated emotional wounds and self-sabotage.
- Practice vulnerability by opening up about your truths with those closest to you.

What meaningful EQ goals excite you? Mapping long-term plans engages you in the lifelong journey ahead.

Lifelong Development

_*"Everyone thinks of changing the world, but no one thinks of changing himself."* - Leo Tolstoy

The greatest emotional intelligence masters view growth as a never-ending road. They avoid complacency once reaching a certain level of skill or success.

Be wary of the following traps as you advance on your EQ journey:

- **Plateaus** - Feeling you have "*arrived*" rather than pushing your abilities further. Remember capacities like empathy have no ceiling.
- **Willpower fatigue** - Letting daily practices lapse after the initial motivation fades. Build long-term intrinsic rewards.
- **Self-concealment** - Downplaying your weaknesses or socially conforming rather than embracing vulnerability and authenticity.
- **Forgetting foundations** - Becoming so focused on advanced techniques you overlook core practices like connection, compassion, and integrity.

Avoid burnout and remain humble by returning regularly to the EQ fundamentals. Measure growth not by achievements, but by your commitment to keep evolving each day. The emotional intelligence journey never truly ends!

Chapter 6 - Key Points

- Review the core principles and practices from each chapter to integrate emotional intelligence fully.
- Daily rituals build EQ through reflection, self-care, interpersonal connection, reading, mindfulness, and savoring life's gifts.
- Set long-term goals that progressively stretch your empathy, self-understanding, leadership impact, and emotional wisdom.
- Sustain motivation and inspiration by focusing on the journey, not just achievements. Keep growing and learning.
- Savor both your accomplishments and efforts expended. Remember to nourish yourself along the demanding path of growth.

Chapter 6 - Reflection Questions

- What are your next steps, both short-term and long-term, to keep elevating your EQ?
- What practices and rituals from this book resonated most powerfully for you? How will you incorporate them moving forward?
- How will you sustain emotional intelligence growth when motivation inevitably fluctuates? Who or what will inspire you along the way?

And with that, my friend, you have all the tools needed to traverse your unique path to emotional intelligence mastery. I wish you profound wisdom, compassion, happiness, and fulfillment on the road ahead. Keep shining your inner light!

Conclusion

We have now completed a life-changing journey together exploring the terrain of emotional intelligence. By taking the time to read this book, you have demonstrated your dedication to self-improvement and willingness to walk the challenging but rewarding path to mastery.

In the introduction, I described emotional intelligence as the capacity to perceive, understand, regulate, and harness emotions adaptively. We discussed how developing EQ offers immense benefits for your relationships, leadership, mental health, physical health, performance, and overall life satisfaction.

While some individuals possess innate emotional sensitivity, EQ skills can be deliberately cultivated through knowledge, self-reflection, and applied practice. This book provided you research-backed frameworks, tools, and exercises to help construct your customized pathway to mastery.

Journey of Self-Discovery

The first leg of our journey focused on intrapersonal intelligence - your inner world. In Chapter 1, you learned the evolutionary origins and purposes behind emotions. We explored your characteristic emotional patterns, biases, and beliefs. Building this self-awareness provides the foundation to then regulate unhelpful emotions more consciously.

Chapter 2 equipped you with science-based strategies to manage destructive emotions skillfully and defuse from emotional mind back into rational mind. You can break longstanding destructive habits through purposeful practice. Emotional agility emerges as you gain the flexibility to shift mindsets fluidly based on the situation.

Harnessing emotions for motivation powered by your deepest values filled Chapter 3. Rather than chasing fleeting external validation, you can derive internal strength from discovering your unique purpose and living your eulogy virtues each day. Lifting others up along the way adds meaning.

Expanding Your Circle of Compassion

In the second half of our journey, we expanded focus to apply emotional intelligence to relationships. Chapter 4 discussed empathy, including both understanding others' perspectives cognitively and connecting emotionally. You learned techniques like vulnerable sharing, loving-kindness meditation, and reading diverse literature to expand your circle of compassion.

Armed with emotional attunement and empathy, Chapter 5 highlighted using EQ to enrich your communication, resolve conflict cooperatively, provide constructive feedback, and influence people through inspiration. Storytelling that stirs hearts as well as minds makes leadership emotionally compelling.

Finally, Chapter 6 encouraged you to review all the mindsets, skills, and practices gleaned along the way. I offered suggestions for daily EQ rituals to make emotional intelligence second nature. You set ambitious long-term goals for how to keep advancing your capacities over the years ahead.

Live With Emotional Wisdom

The ultimate aim of emotional intelligence is achieving emotional wisdom. This means applying your understanding of emotions, empathy, and knowledge of human nature to make optimal decisions - for yourself, your relationships, and society. Emotional wisdom should guide you as citizen, neighbor, partner, parent, and leader.

I hope this book provided a foundation and roadmap as you continue on the lifelong path to mastering your emotions, realizing your potential, and serving the world. Keep growing in self-understanding, courage, compassion, and integrity. We all face ups and downs, but challenges become opportunities when you approach life with emotional intelligence.

I am confident that the lessons you internalized have equipped you with strength to live more purposefully and overcome obstacles that once held you back. Your only limitations now are the ones you set yourself. Let your reach perpetually exceed your grasp.

Many blessings to you, my fellow traveler. May your journey unfold with increasing insight, connection, fulfillment, and emotional wisdom. This community stands behind you along the way. Now venture forth and shine your light fully! The greatest gift you can offer the world is your own emotional intelligence.

About the Author

Monday Farouq's path to becoming an expert in emotions and well-being has been an unconventional one, guided by both personal experience and his desire to help others.

Raised in a family that struggled with emotional health issues, Monday saw firsthand the toll that unmanaged emotions can take. The pain and confusion he observed in loved ones lit a passion within him to better understand the complexities of the human mind and heart.

This early exposure to mental health challenges inspired Monday to pursue psychology in college and beyond. But he has never lost touch with the human side of healing. Monday gravitates toward the raw, messy reality people face in their inner worlds and relationships.

Over years counseling clients and teaching students, Monday retained his humility even as he earned professional accolades. He believes true emotional wisdom comes not from academic knowledge alone, but from supporting real people through mental and physical rehabilitation.

Monday brings insatiable curiosity to his work, always expanding his expertise through research, training, and collaborating with fellow experts worldwide. Yet he distills his learnings into accessible guidance for everyday people trying to navigate life's ups and downs.

Above all, Monday radiates a spirit of compassion. He believes in every person's potential for emotional growth and fulfillment with the right support and tools. This book reflects his caring approach - meeting you wherever you are and empowering your journey.

To Monday, being an author means serving people through hard-won but often simple wisdom. By sharing his knowledge and experiences, he hopes to shed light on the path to mastery and well-being for anyone willing to learn. That has been his life's purpose and privilege.

www.ingramcontent.com/pod-product-compliance
Lightning Source LLC
Chambersburg PA
CBHW071056260726
48661CB00006B/2304